# REMOTE WORK MASTERY: MANAGING STRESS AND OVERCOMING CHALLENGES.

## RAYAN D'ARCY

RAYAN D'ARCY
HOW TO ACHIEVE AESTHETIC

Copyright © 2024 by Rayan D'Arcy

All Rights Reserved: No part of this book may be reproduced, distributed, or transmitted in any form or by any means, including photocopying, recording, or other electronic or mechanical methods, without the prior written permission of the publisher.

**THIS BOOK BLONGS TO :**

_____

# TABLE OF CONTENTS

| | |
|---|---|
| Introduction | 2 |
| Chapter 1: Embracing the Remote Work Lifestyle | 6 |
| Chapter 2: Identifying and Managing Stress | 16 |
| Chapter 3: Creating a Productive Workspace | 24 |
| Chapter 4: Crafting Effective Daily Routines | 31 |
| Chapter 5: Mastering Time Management | 39 |
| Chapter 6: Insights and Success Stories | 46 |
| Chapter 7: Establishing Healthy Boundaries | 52 |
| Chapter 8: Enhancing Mental Health and Well-Being | 62 |
| Chapter 9: Staying Connected and Engaged | 69 |
| Chapter 10: Managing Workload and Expectations | 76 |
| Conclusion | 81 |
| BIBLIOGRAPHY | 83 |

# INTRODUCTION

**Welcome to Remote Work Mastery:**
Imagine starting your day with a fresh cup of coffee, setting up your workspace at home, and diving into your tasks without the hassle of a morning commute. This is the new reality for millions of people around the globe who have embraced remote work. While the flexibility and freedom of working from home are undeniable perks, they also come with unique challenges. This book, "Remote Work Mastery: Managing Stress and Overcoming Challenges," is your guide to navigating these challenges and thriving in your remote work environment.

**The Remote Work Revolution:**
The shift to remote work has been nothing short of revolutionary. It has transformed how we think about our professional lives, offering unprecedented flexibility and control over our schedules. No more battling traffic or being confined to a cubicle. Instead, we have the autonomy to design our workdays around our personal lives. But with this freedom comes a set of new stressors and obstacles that can impact our productivity and well-being.

**Understanding the Unique Challenges:**

Working remotely means facing isolation from colleagues, blurred boundaries between work and personal life, and the pressure to always be available. These factors can lead to increased stress, burnout, and a feeling of being overwhelmed. The lack of physical separation between your workspace and personal space can make it difficult to switch off from work mode, leading to longer hours and less downtime.

**Why This Book Matters:**

This book is designed to help you master the art of remote work by addressing both the stress management and broader challenges you may face. Whether you're a seasoned remote worker or new to this lifestyle, you'll find valuable insights and practical advice to help you succeed. From creating a productive workspace to setting healthy boundaries and managing your workload, this book covers it all.

**What You'll Find Inside:**

In "Remote Work Mastery: Managing Stress and Overcoming Challenges," you'll discover a treasure trove of practical strategies and actionable advice tailored specifically for remote workers. Each chapter is designed to provide comprehensive coverage of all aspects of remote work, from setting up an efficient and comfortable home office to mastering the art of time management. The book takes a holistic approach, focusing not only on productivity but also on maintaining mental, physical, and emotional well-being. You'll learn how to create healthy daily routines, set clear boundaries, and manage stress effectively. With real-world insights and success stories from seasoned remote workers, you'll gain valuable perspectives and techniques to enhance your remote work experience. Additionally, the book offers tools and techniques to help you stay connected and engaged with your team, navigate career growth, and overcome the isolation often associated with remote work. By following the guidance in this book, you'll be well-equipped to handle the challenges of remote work and transform them into opportunities for personal and professional growth.

**Your Ultimate Remote Work Companion:**
Packed with practical strategies, actionable advice, and real-world insights, this book is your go-to resource for navigating the unique challenges of remote work. Whether you're managing stress, creating the perfect home office, or finding a healthy work-life balance, you'll discover everything you need to excel and thrive in your remote work journey.

**Let's Get Started:**

So, grab your coffee, find your favorite spot, and let's dive into the world of remote work mastery. Together, we'll turn the challenges of remote work into opportunities for growth and well-being. Welcome to your new work-life balance.

# CHAPTER 1: EMBRACING THE REMOTE WORK LIFESTYLE

The remote work revolution has dramatically transformed the landscape of professional life. What was once a rare privilege has now become a norm for millions around the world. This shift offers numerous advantages, from increased flexibility to significant cost savings, but it also brings unique challenges that require careful navigation. This chapter explores the benefits and challenges of remote work, providing a comprehensive guide to transitioning from office life to working from home, setting up a productive workspace, and cultivating the right mindset for success.

## Understanding the Remote Work Revolution:

The digital age has catalyzed a significant shift in how we approach work. Advancements in technology, such as high-speed internet, cloud computing, and sophisticated communication tools, have made it possible for many jobs to be performed remotely. This transformation was accelerated by global events like the COVID-19 pandemic, which forced many organizations to adopt remote work models to ensure business continuity. The benefits of this transition are numerous, but so are the challenges. Understanding both is crucial for anyone looking to thrive in a remote work environment.

## 1-The Benefits of Remote Work:

### 1-1 Flexibility and Autonomy:
**Work-Life Balance:** One of the most lauded benefits of remote work is the ability to create a schedule that fits your lifestyle. This flexibility allows you to work during your most productive hours and attend to personal responsibilities more easily.

**Increased Autonomy:** Remote work empowers employees to take charge of their own schedules and work environments, fostering a sense of independence and responsibility.

### 1-2 Elimination of Commutes:
**Time Savings:** The average American spends about 26 minutes commuting each way, adding up to over 200 hours a year. Remote work eliminates this time drain, allowing for more productive and personal activities.

**Reduced Stress:** Commuting can be a significant source of stress due to traffic, delays, and the hustle and bustle of public transport. Removing this daily burden can greatly enhance your overall well-being.

### 1-3 Cost Savings:
**For Employees:** Remote workers save money on transportation, work attire, and daily meals. These savings can be substantial, especially in expensive urban areas.

**For Employers:** Companies can reduce overhead costs associated with maintaining physical office spaces, such as rent, utilities, and office supplies.

## 1-4 Increased Productivity:
**Fewer Distractions:** Many remote workers find they are more productive at home due to fewer interruptions from colleagues and a quieter work environment.

**Customized Work Environment:** Employees can tailor their workspaces to their preferences, enhancing comfort and efficiency.

## 1-5 Access to a Global Talent Pool:
**Diverse Perspectives:** Hiring remote employees allows companies to access a broader range of skills and perspectives, fostering innovation and creativity.

**Geographic Flexibility:** Organizations are no longer limited by geographic boundaries, enabling them to hire the best talent from around the world.

## 2-The Challenges of Remote Work:

## 2-1 Isolation and Loneliness:
**Social Interaction:** The lack of in-person interaction can lead to feelings of isolation and loneliness. Remote workers miss out on the social aspects of office life, such as casual conversations and team lunches.

**Mental Health Impact:** Prolonged isolation can negatively affect mental health, leading to depression and anxiety if not properly managed.

## 2-2 Blurring of Boundaries:

**Work-Life Integration:** Without a clear separation between work and personal life, remote workers may struggle to disconnect from work, leading to longer hours and burnout.

**Physical Space:** Working in the same space where you relax can make it difficult to switch off from work mode, impacting both productivity and relaxation.

## 2-3 Communication Barriers:

**Digital Communication:** Remote work relies heavily on digital communication, which can sometimes lead to misunderstandings or a lack of clarity. Effective communication requires deliberate effort and the right tools.

**Cultural Differences:** Working with a global team means navigating different time zones, languages, and cultural norms, which can complicate collaboration.

## 2-4 Distractions at Home:

**Household Interruptions:** Family members, pets, and household chores can be significant distractions when working from home.

**Creating Boundaries:** Establishing a dedicated workspace and setting boundaries with those you live with is crucial to minimize interruptions.

## 2-5 Technical Issues:

**Reliability of Technology:** Remote work is heavily dependent on technology. Internet outages, software glitches, and hardware failures can disrupt work and cause frustration.

**Security Concerns:** Working remotely can pose cybersecurity risks, requiring robust measures to protect sensitive information.

## 3-Transitioning from Office to Home:

Making a successful transition to remote work involves more than just setting up a home office. It requires a shift in mindset and the development of new habits and routines. Here are some steps to help make this transition smoother:

## 3-1 Set Up a Dedicated Workspace:

**Choose the Right Spot:** Select a quiet, comfortable area in your home that can be dedicated to work. This helps create a physical boundary between work and personal life.

**Invest in Ergonomics:** Ensure your workspace is ergonomically designed to prevent strain and injury. A good chair, proper desk height, and appropriate lighting are essential.

**Minimize Distractions:** Set up your workspace in a low-traffic area of your home to reduce interruptions. Use noise-canceling headphones if necessary.

## 3-2 Establish a Routine:

**Create a Daily Schedule:** Develop a consistent daily routine that includes set work hours, regular breaks, and time for personal activities. Consistency helps maintain a sense of normalcy and productivity.

**Morning Rituals:** Start your day with a morning ritual that prepares you mentally and physically for work. This could include exercise, meditation, or simply having breakfast.

**End-of-Day Rituals:** Signal the end of your workday with a ritual that helps you transition from work to personal time. This could be a walk, a workout, or spending time with family.

## 3-3 Invest in the Right Tools:

**Technology Essentials:** Ensure you have the necessary technology to perform your job effectively. This includes a reliable computer, high-speed internet, and communication and collaboration software.

**Software and Apps:** Use productivity tools like task managers, calendars, and project management software to stay organized and on track.

## 3-4 Communicate Clearly and Frequently:

**Regular Check-Ins:** Stay connected with your team through regular check-ins, video calls, and instant messaging. Clear communication is key to maintaining collaboration and avoiding misunderstandings.

**Use Multiple Channels:** Leverage various communication tools such as email, chat, and video conferencing to ensure messages are conveyed effectively.

## 3-5 Set Boundaries:
**Define Work Hours:** Clearly define your work hours and communicate them to family members or housemates. Let them know when you should not be disturbed to minimize distractions.

**Personal Time:** Ensure you allocate time for personal activities and relaxation. Avoid the temptation to overwork and respect your own boundaries.

## 4-Setting the Right Mindset:

Embracing a remote work lifestyle also involves cultivating the right mindset. Here are some strategies to help you stay positive and productive:

## 4-1 Stay Organized:
**Task Management:** Keep track of your tasks and deadlines using digital tools or planners. Prioritize your work and break tasks into manageable chunks to avoid feeling overwhelmed.

**Declutter:** Keep your workspace tidy and organized to minimize distractions and enhance focus.

## 4-2 Take Care of Your Mental and Physical Health:

**Exercise Regularly:** Incorporate physical activity into your daily routine to reduce stress and boost energy levels. Even short breaks for stretching or walking can make a difference.

**Healthy Eating:** Maintain a balanced diet and stay hydrated. Avoid the temptation of unhealthy snacks and prioritize nutritious meals.

**Mindfulness Practices:** Practice mindfulness and meditation to manage stress and improve focus. Techniques such as deep breathing and guided meditation can be beneficial.

## 4-3 Stay Social:

**Virtual Socializing:** Make an effort to stay connected with colleagues and friends. Virtual coffee breaks, online chats, and video calls can help mitigate feelings of isolation.

**Join Communities:** Engage with online communities and forums related to your interests or profession to build connections and find support.

## 4-4 Continuous Learning:

**Professional Development:** Take advantage of online courses and resources to continue developing your skills and knowledge. This not only keeps you engaged but also enhances your career prospects.

**Stay Informed:** Keep up with industry trends and news to stay relevant and informed about your field.

**4-5 Celebrate Successes:**

**Acknowledge Achievements:** Acknowledge and celebrate your achievements, no matter how small. This helps boost morale and keeps you motivated.

**Reward Yourself:** Treat yourself to small rewards for completing tasks or reaching milestones. This can help maintain motivation and make work more enjoyable.

Transitioning to a remote work lifestyle is a significant change that comes with its own set of benefits and challenges. By understanding these dynamics and implementing effective strategies, you can make the most of this flexible work arrangement. In the following chapters, we will delve deeper into specific aspects of remote work, offering practical advice and solutions to help you thrive in your remote work journey.

# CHAPTER 2: IDENTIFYING AND MANAGING STRESS

Stress is an inevitable part of life, but the unique challenges of remote work can amplify stress levels if not managed properly. The shift to working from home offers flexibility and freedom but also introduces new stressors that can significantly impact your well-being. Identifying the specific stressors that affect you as a remote worker is the first step toward effective stress management. This chapter will guide you through recognizing these stressors and provide practical strategies to manage and mitigate them, helping you maintain a healthy, productive remote work environment.

## Understanding Stress in Remote Work:

Remote work blurs the boundaries between personal and professional life, leading to a sense of being always "on call" and unable to fully disconnect. The constant connectivity can increase stress levels as the line between work hours and personal time becomes increasingly vague. Additionally, isolation from colleagues and the lack of face-to-face interactions can lead to feelings of loneliness and disconnection, further exacerbating stress.

Stress in the context of remote work can be multifaceted. It can stem from the isolation of working alone, the pressure to always be available, or the difficulty in separating work life from personal life. Recognizing these stressors allows you to develop targeted strategies to address them, reducing their impact on your mental and physical health.

## 1-Common Stressors for Remote Workers:

### 1-1 Isolation and Loneliness:
**Lack of Social Interaction:** Remote workers often miss out on the social interactions that come naturally in an office environment. This can lead to feelings of loneliness and disconnection.

**Emotional Impact:** Prolonged isolation can negatively impact mental health, leading to anxiety and depression if not addressed.

### 1-2 Blurred Boundaries:
**Work-Life Balance:** Without a clear separation between work and personal life, remote workers may find themselves working longer hours, leading to burnout.

**Physical Boundaries:** Working in a space meant for relaxation can make it difficult to switch off from work mode, impacting both productivity and personal time.

### 1-3 Communication Challenges:
**Misunderstandings:** Reliance on digital communication can sometimes lead to misunderstandings or a lack of clarity, causing frustration and stress.

**Time Zones:** Working with a global team can present challenges in coordinating meetings and deadlines, leading to increased stress.

### 1-4 Distractions at Home:
**Family and Household:** Balancing work with household responsibilities and family demands can be challenging, leading to interruptions and reduced productivity.
**Lack of Routine:** Without a structured routine, it can be easy to get distracted by non-work-related activities.

### 1-5 Technical Issues:
**Technology Dependence:** Remote work relies heavily on technology. Internet outages, software malfunctions, and other technical issues can disrupt work and cause stress.
**Cybersecurity:** Ensuring the security of work-related information and maintaining data privacy can add to the stress of remote working.

## 2-Self-Assessment Tools for Stress:

Understanding your personal stress triggers is essential for effective management. Here are some self-assessment tools to help you identify your stressors:

### 2-1 Daily Stress Log:
**Track Your Stress:** Keep a daily log of situations that cause you stress. Note the time, the trigger, your reaction, and how you managed it.
**Identify Patterns:** After a week or two, review your log to identify patterns and common triggers.

## 2-2 Stress Inventory Questionnaires:
**Professional Assessments:** Use validated stress inventory questionnaires such as the Perceived Stress Scale (PSS) or the Holmes-Rahe Stress Inventory to gauge your stress levels.

**Self-Reflection:** Reflect on the results to understand the primary sources of your stress.

## 2-3 Physical and Emotional Symptoms Checklist:
**Recognize Symptoms:** Create a checklist of physical and emotional symptoms associated with stress, such as headaches, fatigue, irritability, and anxiety.

**Monitor Regularly:** Regularly check in with yourself to monitor these symptoms and note any changes.

## 3-Strategies for Immediate Stress Relief:

Once you've identified your stressors, the next step is to implement strategies to manage and mitigate them. Here are practical techniques for immediate stress relief:

## 3-1 Breathing Exercises:
**Deep Breathing:** Practice deep breathing exercises to calm your nervous system. Inhale slowly through your nose, hold for a few seconds, and exhale slowly through your mouth.

**Box Breathing:** Try box breathing by inhaling for four seconds, holding your breath for four seconds, exhaling for four seconds, and holding again for four seconds.

### 3-2 Mindfulness and Meditation:

**Mindfulness Practices:** Engage in mindfulness practices to stay present and reduce anxiety. Apps like Headspace and Calm offer guided sessions.

**Meditation Techniques:** Set aside time each day for meditation. Even a few minutes can help reduce stress and improve focus.

### 3-3 Physical Activity:

**Exercise Regularly:** Incorporate physical activity into your daily routine. Exercise releases endorphins, which help reduce stress.

**Stretching and Yoga:** Take breaks to stretch or practice yoga. These activities can relieve physical tension and promote relaxation.

### 3-4 Time Management:

**Prioritize Tasks:** Use tools like the Eisenhower Matrix to prioritize tasks based on their urgency and importance.

**Break Tasks into Chunks:** Break larger tasks into smaller, manageable steps to avoid feeling overwhelmed.

### 3-5 Healthy Lifestyle Choices:

**Balanced Diet:** Maintain a healthy diet to support your physical and mental well-being. Avoid excessive caffeine and sugar, which can increase stress levels.

**Adequate Sleep:** Ensure you get enough sleep each night. Establish a regular sleep schedule and create a relaxing bedtime routine.

## 4-Creating a Long-Term Stress Management Plan:

While immediate stress relief techniques are essential, developing a long-term stress management plan is equally important. Here are steps to create a sustainable plan:

### 4-1 Set Realistic Goals:
**Short-Term and Long-Term Goals:** Define both short-term and long-term goals for your personal and professional life. Ensure they are realistic and attainable.
**Regular Review:** Regularly review and adjust your goals as needed to stay on track and reduce stress.

### 4-2 Develop a Support Network:
**Professional Support:** Seek support from colleagues, supervisors, or professional counselors. Don't hesitate to ask for help when needed.
**Social Connections:** Maintain strong social connections with friends and family. Regular social interactions can provide emotional support and reduce feelings of isolation.

### 4-3 Implement Regular Self-Care Practices:
**Scheduled Downtime:** Schedule regular downtime to relax and recharge. Engage in activities you enjoy, such as reading, hobbies, or spending time outdoors.

**Self-Compassion:** Practice self-compassion and be kind to yourself. Acknowledge your achievements and avoid self-criticism.

## 4-4 Continuous Learning and Adaptation:

**Stay Informed:** Keep up with the latest research and best practices in stress management and remote work. Continuously adapt your strategies as needed.

**Professional Development:** Invest in your professional development through online courses, workshops, and training. Enhancing your skills can boost your confidence and reduce work-related stress.


Managing stress in a remote work environment requires a proactive and holistic approach. By identifying your unique stressors and implementing both immediate and long-term strategies, you can create a healthier, more productive remote work experience. In the next chapter, we will explore how to create a productive workspace that supports your well-being and enhances your efficiency.

# CHAPTER 3: CREATING A PRODUCTIVE WORKSPACE

A well-designed workspace is essential for maintaining productivity and reducing stress while working remotely. Unlike traditional office environments, remote workspaces must be tailored to fit individual needs and preferences. This chapter will guide you through setting up a productive workspace, focusing on ergonomics, technology, and organization to create an environment that supports your well-being and efficiency.

## 1-Designing Your Home Office:

Creating an effective home office involves more than just finding a place to set your laptop. It requires thoughtful planning to ensure that your workspace promotes productivity and minimizes distractions.

### 1-1 Choosing the Right Location:

**Quiet and Private:** Select a quiet area of your home where you can work without interruptions. If possible, choose a space with a door to separate your work environment from the rest of the household.

**Natural Light:** Position your workspace near a window to take advantage of natural light, which can boost your mood and energy levels. Ensure that the light does not create glare on your screen.

**Adequate Space:** Ensure you have enough space for all your work materials and equipment. A cramped workspace can lead to discomfort and decreased productivity.

## 1-2 Essential Furniture and Equipment:

**Ergonomic Chair:** Invest in a high-quality ergonomic chair that provides proper support for your back and promotes good posture. A comfortable chair can prevent back pain and improve your focus.

**Adjustable Desk:** Consider a desk that allows you to adjust the height or switch between sitting and standing positions. This flexibility can reduce the strain on your body and improve circulation.

**Proper Lighting:** Use a combination of natural and artificial lighting to create a well-lit workspace. A desk lamp with adjustable brightness can help reduce eye strain.

**Organizational Tools:** Keep your workspace organized with shelves, filing cabinets, and desk organizers. A clutter-free environment can enhance your focus and efficiency.

## 1-3 Technology and Tools:

**Reliable Internet Connection:** Ensure you have a high-speed internet connection to support video calls, file transfers, and other online activities. Consider using a wired connection for greater stability.

**Computer and Peripherals:** Invest in a reliable computer with the necessary specifications for your work. Additional peripherals, such as an external monitor, keyboard, and mouse, can enhance your comfort and productivity.

**Software and Applications:** Utilize productivity tools and applications that help you stay organized and connected. Project management software, communication tools, and time-tracking apps can streamline your workflow.

**Backup Solutions:** Implement regular data backup solutions to protect your work. Use cloud storage or an external hard drive to ensure your files are safe and accessible.

## 2-Ergonomics and Comfort:

Ergonomics plays a crucial role in preventing physical discomfort and injuries associated with prolonged sitting and computer use. Setting up your workspace ergonomically can improve your posture, reduce strain, and enhance overall comfort.

### 2-1 Ergonomic Setup:

**Monitor Position:** Position your monitor at eye level, about an arm's length away, to reduce neck and eye strain. Use a monitor stand or stack books to achieve the right height.

**Chair and Desk Height:** Adjust your chair and desk so that your feet are flat on the floor, your knees are at a 90-degree angle, and your elbows are at the same height as the desk. This setup promotes a neutral posture and reduces strain on your back and shoulders.

**Keyboard and Mouse Placement:** Place your keyboard and mouse within easy reach, allowing your arms to remain relaxed and close to your body. Use a wrist rest to support your wrists and prevent strain.

## 2-2 Taking Breaks and Stretching:

**Regular Breaks:** Take short breaks every hour to stand up, stretch, and move around. This practice can reduce fatigue and improve circulation.
Stretching Exercises: Incorporate stretching exercises into your routine to relieve muscle tension and prevent stiffness. Focus on stretches that target your neck, shoulders, back, and legs.
**Standing Desk Options:** Consider using a standing desk or a desk converter to alternate between sitting and standing throughout the day. This change in position can reduce the negative effects of prolonged sitting.

## 3-Ergonomic Setup:

An organized workspace is key to maintaining productivity and reducing stress. By keeping your environment tidy and well-organized, you can focus better and work more efficiently.

## 3-1 Decluttering Your Workspace:
**Minimalist Approach:** Adopt a minimalist approach to your workspace by keeping only essential items on your desk. This reduces visual clutter and distractions.

**Regular Cleaning:** Make it a habit to clean and organize your workspace regularly. Dispose of unnecessary items, file documents properly, and wipe down surfaces to maintain a clean environment.

**Cable Management:** Use cable organizers or clips to keep cords and cables neatly arranged. This prevents tangling and makes your workspace look more orderly.

## 3-2 Time Management and Productivity:

**Task Lists:** Create daily or weekly task lists to keep track of your responsibilities and prioritize your work. Use digital tools or planners to stay organized.

**Time Blocking:** Implement time-blocking techniques to allocate specific periods for different tasks. This helps you stay focused and manage your time effectively.

**Productivity Techniques:** Experiment with productivity techniques such as the Pomodoro Technique, where you work for a set period and take short breaks in between. This can enhance concentration and prevent burnout.

## 3-3 Personalizing Your Workspace:

**Inspiring Decor:** Personalize your workspace with items that inspire and motivate you, such as artwork, plants, or photographs. A personalized environment can boost your mood and creativity.

**Comfort Items:** Include items that contribute to your comfort, such as a cozy blanket, a favorite mug, or a diffuser with calming scents. These small touches can make your workspace more enjoyable.

Creating a productive and comfortable workspace is essential for success in remote work. A thoughtfully designed home office that prioritizes ergonomics and organization can significantly enhance your productivity and well-being. By investing time and effort into setting up a dedicated workspace, you can create an environment that supports your professional goals and personal comfort. An ergonomic setup helps prevent physical discomfort and injuries, while a well-organized space minimizes distractions and boosts efficiency. Personalizing your workspace with inspiring decor and comfort items can also improve your mood and motivation.

In the next chapter, we will explore how to craft effective daily routines to enhance your productivity and well-being. Establishing structured routines is crucial for remote workers to kickstart their day positively, maintain momentum throughout work hours, and wind down effectively in the evening. By developing consistent morning rituals, incorporating regular breaks, and ending your day with calming activities, you can create a harmonious balance that supports your overall well-being and productivity.

# CHAPTER 4: CRAFTING EFFECTIVE DAILY ROUTINES

Creating effective daily routines is a cornerstone of productivity and well-being for remote workers. A well-structured day helps maintain focus, reduce stress, and enhance work-life balance. This chapter will guide you through developing routines that kickstart your day, sustain productivity during work hours, and help you wind down in the evening. By incorporating these routines, you can optimize your workday, minimize distractions, and ensure a healthy, balanced lifestyle.

## 1-Morning Routines to Kickstart Your Day:

Starting your day with a consistent morning routine sets a positive tone for the rest of your day. It prepares your mind and body for the tasks ahead and helps establish a sense of normalcy and structure.

### 1-1 Wake Up at the Same Time:
**Consistency:** Aim to wake up at the same time every day, even on weekends. Consistent wake-up times regulate your body's internal clock and improve sleep quality.
**Morning Light Exposure:** Expose yourself to natural light soon after waking up. Natural light helps signal to your body that it's time to be awake and alert, boosting your energy levels.

## 1-2 Mindful Mornings:

**Mindfulness Practice:** Start your day with mindfulness practices such as meditation, deep breathing, or journaling. These practices can help center your thoughts and reduce stress.

**Gratitude Journaling:** Spend a few minutes writing down things you are grateful for. This can shift your mindset to a positive outlook and set a constructive tone for the day.

## 1-3 Physical Activity:

**Exercise Routine:** Incorporate physical activity into your morning routine. This could be a full workout, yoga session, or a brisk walk. Exercise boosts endorphins and energy levels.

**Stretching:** If a full workout isn't feasible, spend a few minutes stretching. Stretching helps increase blood flow and flexibility, preparing your body for the day.

## 1-4 Nutritious Breakfast:

**Healthy Eating:** Fuel your body with a nutritious breakfast. Opt for balanced meals that include protein, whole grains, and fruits or vegetables. A healthy breakfast provides sustained energy and improves concentration.

**Hydration:** Start your day with a glass of water to rehydrate after sleep. Staying hydrated is crucial for maintaining energy levels and cognitive function.

## 1-5 Planning Your Day:

**Set Priorities:** Take a few minutes to outline your tasks and priorities for the day. This can help you stay focused and organized.

**Visualize Success:** Spend a moment visualizing a successful day. Positive visualization can boost your motivation and confidence.

## 2-Midday Breaks and Productivity Boosters:

Maintaining productivity throughout the day requires strategic breaks and activities that keep you energized and focused.

## 2-1 Scheduled Breaks:

**Pomodoro Technique:** Use the Pomodoro Technique, which involves working for 25 minutes and then taking a 5-minute break. This method helps maintain focus and prevents burnout.

**Longer Breaks:** Incorporate longer breaks, such as a lunch break, where you step away from your workspace and recharge. Use this time to relax, eat a nutritious meal, and perhaps take a short walk.

## 2-2 Movement and Exercise:

**Mini Workouts:** Integrate short bursts of physical activity into your breaks. Activities like stretching, desk exercises, or a quick walk can help refresh your mind and body.

**Standing Breaks:** If you use a standing desk, alternate between sitting and standing to reduce physical strain and increase circulation.

## 2-3 Mindfulness and Relaxation:

**Breathing Exercises:** Practice deep breathing exercises during breaks to reduce stress and refocus. Inhale deeply, hold for a few seconds, and exhale slowly.

**Quick Meditations:** Use guided meditation apps for short, 5-10 minute sessions to clear your mind and reduce anxiety.

## 2-4 Healthy Snacking:

**Nutrient-Dense Snacks:** Choose snacks that provide lasting energy, such as nuts, fruits, or yogurt. Avoid sugary snacks that can lead to energy crashes.

**Stay Hydrated:** Keep a water bottle at your desk and drink regularly throughout the day to stay hydrated and maintain focus.

## 2-5 Productivity Boosters:

**Task Switching:** If you feel stuck on a particular task, switch to a different one for a while. This can help refresh your perspective and boost creativity.

**Environment Changes:** Change your environment briefly by moving to a different room or stepping outside. A change of scenery can reinvigorate your mind.

## 2-3 Social Interactions:
**Virtual Coffee Breaks:** Schedule short, informal video calls with colleagues to catch up and share experiences. This can reduce feelings of isolation and foster a sense of community.
**Networking Opportunities:** Use breaks to engage with professional communities or social media groups related to your field. Building connections can provide support and inspiration.

## 3-End-of-Day Rituals to Wind Down:

Ending your workday with a consistent routine helps signal to your body and mind that it's time to transition from work to personal time. This practice promotes relaxation and improves work-life balance.

## 3-1 Clear Your Workspace:
**Tidy Up:** Spend a few minutes organizing your workspace. A clean and orderly environment can help you start the next day with a clear mind.
**End-of-Day Review:** Reflect on what you accomplished and create a to-do list for the next day. This can help you leave work-related thoughts at your desk and reduce anxiety about unfinished tasks.

## 3-2 Transition Activities:
**Change of Environment:** Physically move away from your workspace. This separation can help you mentally disconnect from work.

**Evening Exercise:** Engage in light physical activity, such as a walk or yoga, to release any remaining tension and boost endorphins.

## 3-3 Relaxation Techniques:
**Unwind with Hobbies:** Spend time on activities you enjoy, such as reading, cooking, or a creative hobby. Engaging in pleasurable activities can help you relax and recharge.

**Digital Detox:** Limit screen time in the evening, especially from work-related devices. Reducing exposure to blue light can improve sleep quality.

## 3-4 Sleep Preparation:
**Consistent Sleep Schedule:** Aim to go to bed at the same time each night. A regular sleep schedule enhances sleep quality and overall health.

**Relaxing Bedtime Routine:** Create a calming bedtime routine that signals to your body that it's time to sleep. This might include reading, listening to calming music, or practicing gentle stretches.

## 3-5 Reflecting and Unwinding:
**Gratitude and Reflection:** Reflect on the positive aspects of your day and note any achievements or enjoyable moments. This practice can help cultivate a positive mindset and reduce stress.

**Wind-Down Ritual:** Develop a wind-down ritual that helps you relax before bed. This could include a warm bath, meditation, or light stretching.

Crafting effective daily routines is essential for remote workers to maintain productivity, reduce stress, and ensure a healthy work-life balance. By establishing structured morning rituals, incorporating regular breaks, and winding down with end-of-day routines, you can create a harmonious and productive workday. In the next chapter, we will delve into real-world insights and success stories from seasoned remote workers. By learning from their experiences, you will gain practical advice and inspiration to navigate your own remote work journey more effectively. These stories will provide valuable lessons on how to overcome common challenges, enhance productivity, and maintain a healthy work-life balance.

# CHAPTER 5: MASTERING TIME MANAGEMENT

Effective time management is a critical skill for remote workers. With the flexibility of working from home comes the responsibility to manage your own schedule, prioritize tasks, and avoid procrastination. This chapter will explore various strategies and techniques to help you master time management, improve productivity, and achieve a better work-life balance.

## 1-Prioritizing Tasks and Avoiding Procrastination:

One of the biggest challenges in remote work is staying focused and avoiding the temptation to procrastinate. Prioritizing tasks effectively can help you stay on track and make the most of your workday.

### 1-1 Task Prioritization Techniques:
**Eisenhower Matrix:** This method involves categorizing tasks into four quadrants based on their urgency and importance. Focus on tasks that are both urgent and important first, then move on to important but not urgent tasks.

**ABC Method:** Assign each task a priority level: A for high priority, B for medium priority, and C for low priority. Tackle A tasks first, followed by B and C tasks.

**MoSCoW Method:** Prioritize tasks based on whether they are Must-haves, Should-haves, Could-haves, or Won't-haves. This helps you focus on what is most critical.

## 1-2 Avoiding Procrastination:

**Break Tasks into Smaller Steps:** Large tasks can be overwhelming and lead to procrastination. Break them into smaller, manageable steps to make progress easier.

**Set Specific Goals:** Define clear, specific goals for each task. This gives you a clear endpoint to work towards and helps maintain focus.

**Use Time Blocks:** Allocate specific blocks of time for each task or activity. This structure helps keep you on track and prevents tasks from dragging on indefinitely.

## 2-Time Blocking and Scheduling Techniques:

Time blocking is a powerful technique for managing your schedule and ensuring that you allocate sufficient time for both work and personal activities.

## 2-1 Implementing Time Blocking:

**Create a Schedule:** At the beginning of each week, plan your schedule by blocking out time for different tasks and activities. Be sure to include breaks and personal time.

**Stick to Your Blocks:** During each time block, focus solely on the task at hand. Avoid multitasking and distractions to maximize productivity.

**Review and Adjust:** Regularly review your schedule to see what worked and what didn't. Adjust your time blocks as needed to improve efficiency.

## 2-2 Scheduling Techniques:

**Pomodoro Technique:** Work for 25 minutes, then take a 5-minute break. After four cycles, take a longer break. This technique helps maintain focus and prevents burnout.

**90-Minute Work Intervals:** Research suggests that our brains work best in 90-minute intervals. Schedule your work in 90-minute blocks followed by a break.

**Batching Similar Tasks:** Group similar tasks together and tackle them in one block of time. This reduces the cognitive load of switching between different types of tasks.

## 3-Dealing with Distractions:

Working from home comes with its own set of distractions, from household chores to family interruptions. Managing these distractions is key to staying productive.

## 3-1 Minimizing Internal Distractions:

**Designate a Workspace:** Have a dedicated workspace that is free from distractions. This helps signal to your brain that it's time to work.

**Use Noise-Canceling Headphones:** Block out background noise with noise-canceling headphones, especially if you live in a noisy environment.

**Set Boundaries:** Communicate with family members or housemates about your work hours and the importance of minimizing interruptions during those times.

### 3-2 Managing Digital Distractions:

Working from home comes with its own set of distractions, from household chores to family interruptions. Managing these distractions is key to staying productive.

### 3-3 Managing Digital Distractions:

**Turn Off Notifications:** Disable non-essential notifications on your phone and computer. Constant alerts can disrupt your focus.

**Use Website Blockers:** Tools like StayFocusd or Freedom can block distracting websites during work hours.

**Time Management Apps:** Use apps like RescueTime to monitor your digital activity and identify where you might be wasting time.

### 3-4 Creating a Productive Environment:

**Organize Your Workspace:** Keep your workspace tidy and organized. A clutter-free environment can reduce stress and improve focus.

**Ergonomics:** Ensure your workspace is ergonomically designed to prevent physical discomfort and improve your overall work experience.

## 4-Maintaining Work-Life Balance:

Balancing work and personal life is crucial for long-term productivity and well-being. Effective time management helps ensure that both aspects of your life receive the attention they deserve.

### 4-1 Establishing Clear Boundaries:

**Set Work Hours:** Define specific work hours and stick to them. This helps create a clear separation between work and personal time.
**Use a Separate Work Device:** If possible, use a separate device for work and personal activities. This helps reinforce the boundary between work and home life.

### 4-2 Scheduling Personal Time:
**Prioritize Self-Care:** Block out time for self-care activities such as exercise, hobbies, and relaxation. This helps prevent burnout and maintains mental health.
**Plan Social Activities:** Schedule regular social activities to stay connected with friends and family. This can help alleviate feelings of isolation and enhance your well-being.

### 4-3 Regularly Review and Reflect:
**Weekly Review:** At the end of each week, review your time management practices. Reflect on what worked well and what could be improved.

**Adjust Goals:** Adjust your goals and strategies as needed based on your reflections. Continuous improvement is key to mastering time management.

### 4-3 Leveraging Technology for Balance:

**Work-Life Integration Tools:** Utilize tools that help integrate your work and personal life seamlessly. Calendar apps that sync across devices, project management software, and communication platforms can help manage both professional and personal commitments effectively.

**Digital Detox:** Allocate specific times during the day for digital detox, where you completely disconnect from all screens. This practice can help reset your mind and reduce digital fatigue.

Mastering time management is essential for remote workers to stay productive and maintain a healthy work-life balance. By prioritizing tasks, implementing effective scheduling techniques, managing distractions, and maintaining clear boundaries, you can optimize your workday and enhance your overall well-being. In the next chapter, we will delve into real-world insights and success stories from seasoned remote workers. By learning from their experiences, you will gain practical advice and inspiration to navigate your own remote work journey more effectively. These stories will provide valuable lessons on how to overcome common challenges, enhance productivity, and maintain a healthy work-life balance.

# CHAPTER 6: INSIGHTS AND SUCCESS STORIES

Real-world insights and success stories from seasoned remote workers can provide invaluable lessons and inspiration. By learning from their experiences, you can gain practical advice and strategies to navigate your own remote work journey more effectively. This chapter compiles various anecdotes and tips from remote workers who have successfully managed the challenges of working from home, offering a treasure trove of wisdom that can help you enhance your productivity and well-being.

## 1-Real-World Examples of Remote Work Success:

### Example 1: Effective Communication and Team Collaboration:

**Case Study:** Global Marketing Team: A global marketing team spread across different time zones managed to maintain seamless communication and collaboration. They implemented daily stand-up meetings via video calls and used project management tools like Trello and Asana to keep everyone on the same page. This approach ensured that team members were aligned and aware of their tasks, leading to successful project completions.

**Key Takeaway:** Regular communication and the right tools are essential for remote team success. Establishing a routine for check-ins can help maintain clarity and cohesion among team members.

## Example 2: Setting Boundaries and Achieving Work-Life Balance:

**Case Study:** Freelance Graphic Designer: A freelance graphic designer struggled with the temptation to work late into the night. By setting strict work hours and creating a separate office space in their home, they were able to draw a clear line between work and personal time. This change led to improved mental health and increased productivity during working hours.

**Key Takeaway:** Establishing clear boundaries between work and personal life is crucial for preventing burnout and maintaining a healthy balance. Dedicated workspaces and set schedules can help reinforce these boundaries.

## Example 3: Leveraging Technology for Efficiency:

**Case Study: Software Developer:** A software developer found that integrating various productivity tools streamlined their workflow. They used Slack for communication, GitHub for version control, and Zoom for meetings. Automating repetitive tasks with scripts also saved time, allowing them to focus on more complex coding challenges.

**Key Takeaway:** Utilizing technology and automating tasks can significantly enhance efficiency. Choosing the right tools for communication, collaboration, and task management can make a substantial difference in productivity.

**Example 4: Overcoming Isolation and Building Community:**

**Case Study:** Remote Customer Support Specialist: Working alone from home left a customer support specialist feeling isolated. They joined online communities and forums related to their industry and participated in virtual networking events. These interactions provided a sense of community and professional growth, making their remote work experience more fulfilling.

**Key Takeaway:** Combatting isolation is vital for remote workers. Engaging with online communities and participating in virtual events can provide social interaction and professional development opportunities.

## 2-Practical Advice from Seasoned Remote Workers:

### Advice 1: Balancing Flexibility with Structure:

While remote work offers flexibility, maintaining a structured schedule is essential. Set specific work hours, take regular breaks, and stick to your routine as much as possible.

### Advice 2: Creating a Distraction-Free Environment:

Identify and eliminate common distractions in your workspace. This might involve setting boundaries with family members, using noise-canceling headphones, or creating a designated work area that signals it's time to focus.

**Advice 3: Maintaining Professional Development:**
Remote work should not hinder your professional growth. Pursue online courses, attend virtual conferences, and seek out mentorship opportunities to continue advancing your career.

**Advice 4: Fostering Team Morale:**
For managers and team leaders, keeping team morale high is crucial. Regularly recognize and celebrate team achievements, encourage open communication, and provide opportunities for team bonding, even if it's virtual.

## 3-Lessons Learned and Best Practices:

### Lesson 1: Adaptability is Key:
**Insight:** The ability to adapt to changing circumstances is one of the most valuable skills for remote workers. Flexibility in adjusting schedules, workflows, and even personal habits can help manage the unpredictability of remote work.

### Lesson 2: The Importance of Self-Care:
**Insight:** Remote workers must prioritize self-care to maintain their well-being. Regular exercise, healthy eating, and taking time for relaxation and hobbies are essential practices to keep stress levels in check.

### Lesson 3: Continuous Learning:
**Insight:** The remote work landscape is constantly evolving.

Staying updated with new tools, techniques, and industry trends ensures that you remain competitive and effective in your role.

**Lesson 4: Effective Time Management:**
**Insight:** Mastering time management is critical for success in remote work. Techniques such as time blocking, prioritizing tasks, and minimizing distractions can help maintain productivity and work-life balance.

**Lesson 5: Building Strong Virtual Relationships:**
**Insight:** Developing strong relationships with colleagues and supervisors is just as important remotely as it is in-person. Building rapport through regular communication and showing empathy and understanding can foster a supportive work environment.

Learning from the experiences of seasoned remote workers can provide invaluable insights and practical strategies for navigating the challenges of remote work. By applying these lessons, you can enhance your productivity, maintain a healthy work-life balance, and achieve long-term success in your remote work journey. In the next chapter, we will explore how to establish healthy boundaries between work and personal life to prevent burnout and maintain a balanced lifestyle. Setting clear boundaries is crucial for remote workers to avoid the pitfalls of overworking and ensure that both work and personal time are respected.

# CHAPTER 7: ESTABLISHING HEALTHY BOUNDARIES

In the world of remote work, establishing healthy boundaries between professional and personal life is crucial for maintaining productivity and preventing burnout. Without the physical separation of an office, it can be challenging to keep work from encroaching on personal time. This chapter will provide strategies for setting clear boundaries, managing expectations, and ensuring that both work and personal life are respected and balanced.

## 1-Work-Life Balance in a Blended Environment:

Remote work blurs the lines between professional and personal spaces. Creating a balanced environment involves setting clear physical, mental, and temporal boundaries to ensure that work does not dominate your life.

### 1-1 Physical Boundaries:

**Dedicated Workspace:** Establish a specific area in your home that is solely for work. This separation helps create a mental distinction between work and home life.

**Work Zone vs. Relaxation Zone:** Ensure that your work zone is distinct from areas used for relaxation and leisure. This can help you switch off from work mode more effectively at the end of the day.

**Ergonomic Setup:** Invest in ergonomic furniture that supports good posture and reduces physical strain. This setup not only improves productivity but also signals to your brain that it's time for work when you are in this space.

## 1-2 Mental Boundaries:

**Mental Reset Rituals:** Develop routines that signal the start and end of your workday. This could include a short walk, a change of clothes, or a specific activity that helps you transition mentally.

**Mindfulness Practices:** Engage in mindfulness or meditation exercises to help clear your mind and maintain focus. This can reduce stress and improve mental clarity.

**Mental Separation:** Practice mental separation by intentionally focusing on different topics during work and personal time. Use mental cues to switch gears between professional and personal roles.

## 1-3 Temporal Boundaries:

**Set Work Hours:** Define specific work hours and stick to them. Clearly communicate these hours to your colleagues and family to ensure that your work time is respected.

**Breaks and Downtime:** Schedule regular breaks throughout your workday to rest and recharge. Ensure that you also have adequate downtime in the evenings and weekends.

**Protecting Personal Time:** Treat your personal time as sacred and avoid encroaching on it with work-related tasks. This ensures that you have time to unwind and engage in personal activities.

## 2-Setting Clear Work Hours:

Defining and adhering to specific work hours is essential for maintaining a healthy work-life balance. Clear work hours help prevent overworking and ensure that personal time is protected.

### 2-1 Consistent Schedule:
**Regular Hours:** Set regular work hours that mimic a traditional office schedule. This consistency helps you develop a routine and manage your time effectively.

**Communicate Availability:** Clearly communicate your work hours to your team and clients. Use tools like shared calendars to make your availability known and avoid interruptions during personal time.

**Time Awareness:** Use alarms or reminders to signal the start and end of your work hours. This helps you stay mindful of your schedule and avoid the temptation to overwork.

### 2-2 End-of-Day Rituals:
**Daily Wrap-Up:** Establish a ritual to signal the end of your workday, such as shutting down your computer, tidying your workspace, or writing a to-do list for the next day.

**Transition Activities:** Engage in activities that help you transition from work to personal time. This could be a workout, a walk, or spending time with family.

**Unplugging:** Make it a habit to unplug from work-related devices and notifications after work hours to ensure a clear separation between work and personal time.

## 3-Communicating Boundaries with Family and Colleagues:

Effective communication is key to ensuring that your boundaries are understood and respected by both family members and colleagues. Clear and open communication helps manage expectations and reduce conflicts.

### 3-1 With Family:
**Daily Wrap-Up:** Establish a ritual to signal the end of your workday, such as shutting down your computer, tidying your workspace, or writing a to-do list for the next day.
**Transition Activities:** Engage in activities that help you transition from work to personal time. This could be a workout, a walk, or spending time with family.

### 3-2 With Colleagues:
**Set Expectations:** Clearly communicate your work hours and availability to your colleagues. Let them know when you can be reached and when you are off-duty.

**Response Times:** Establish guidelines for response times. Let your team know how quickly you will respond to messages and emails during and outside of work hours.

**Boundary Enforcement:** Politely but firmly enforce your boundaries if colleagues overstep. Reinforce your work hours and the importance of respecting them.

## 3-3 Using Technology:

**Communication Tools:** Use communication tools like Slack, Microsoft Teams, or Zoom to stay connected with your team. Set statuses to indicate your availability and schedule notifications to align with your work hours.

**Work-Life Integration:** Employ tools that help integrate work and personal life without blurring the boundaries, such as scheduling apps that balance both work and personal commitments.

**Automated Responses:** Use automated responses to manage expectations for email and messaging during off-hours. This can help reinforce your boundaries without direct confrontation.

## 4-Dealing with Boundary Violations:

Despite best efforts, boundaries can sometimes be crossed. Knowing how to handle these situations is crucial for maintaining your work-life balance and mental health.

**Response Times:** Establish guidelines for response times. Let your team know how quickly you will respond to messages and emails during and outside of work hours.

**Boundary Enforcement:** Politely but firmly enforce your boundaries if colleagues overstep. Reinforce your work hours and the importance of respecting them.

## 3-3 Using Technology:

**Communication Tools:** Use communication tools like Slack, Microsoft Teams, or Zoom to stay connected with your team. Set statuses to indicate your availability and schedule notifications to align with your work hours.

**Work-Life Integration:** Employ tools that help integrate work and personal life without blurring the boundaries, such as scheduling apps that balance both work and personal commitments.

**Automated Responses:** Use automated responses to manage expectations for email and messaging during off-hours. This can help reinforce your boundaries without direct confrontation.

## 4-Dealing with Boundary Violations:

Despite best efforts, boundaries can sometimes be crossed. Knowing how to handle these situations is crucial for maintaining your work-life balance and mental health.

## 4-1 Addressing Issues with Family:

**Reinforce Boundaries:** Gently remind family members of your work schedule and the importance of uninterrupted work time.

**Seek Compromises:** Find compromises that work for both your professional and personal responsibilities. This might involve adjusting your schedule or finding quiet times for focused work.

**Create Family Agreements:** Develop agreements with family members regarding quiet times, shared spaces, and mutual respect for work commitments.

## 4-2 Addressing Issues with Colleagues:

**Professional Communication:** If a colleague repeatedly interrupts your personal time, address the issue professionally. Reiterate your work hours and the importance of respecting them.

**Escalation:** If the issue persists, consider discussing it with your supervisor or HR to find a resolution that maintains your boundaries.

**Documenting Boundaries:** Keep a record of communications regarding boundaries. This can be useful if the issue needs to be escalated or if there are misunderstandings in the future.

## 5-Building Resilience and Flexibility:

While setting boundaries is crucial, it's also important to remain flexible and resilient. Unexpected events can disrupt even the best-laid plans, and being adaptable can help you navigate these challenges effectively.

## 5-1 Developing Flexibility:

**Adjusting Schedules:** Be open to adjusting your work schedule when necessary, while still maintaining a core structure.

**Adapting to Change:** Develop a mindset that embraces change and seeks solutions rather than dwelling on disruptions.

**Contingency Plans:** Have contingency plans in place for common disruptions, such as internet outages or family emergencies. This can help you respond quickly and effectively.

## 5-2 Building Resilience:

**Stress Management Techniques:** Incorporate stress management techniques into your routine, such as exercise, mindfulness, and hobbies.

**Support Networks:** Build a support network of friends, family, and colleagues who can provide assistance and encouragement during challenging times.

**Self-Care Practices:** Prioritize self-care by regularly engaging in activities that rejuvenate you, whether it's a hobby, spending time in nature, or relaxing with a good book.

Establishing healthy boundaries between work and personal life is essential for remote workers to prevent burnout and maintain a balanced lifestyle. By setting clear physical, mental, and temporal boundaries, communicating effectively with family and colleagues, and dealing with boundary violations professionally, you can create a harmonious balance that supports your overall well-being and productivity. Flexibility and resilience further enhance your ability to manage the dynamic nature of remote work. In the next chapter, we will delve into enhancing mental health and well-being, providing strategies and practices to help you thrive in a remote work environment.

# CHAPTER 8: ENHANCING MENTAL HEALTH AND WELL-BEING

Maintaining mental health and well-being is critical for remote workers. The unique challenges of working from home can impact mental health, making it essential to adopt strategies that promote emotional stability and overall well-being. This chapter explores various techniques and practices to enhance your mental health, ensuring that you can thrive both personally and professionally in a remote work environment.

## 1-Mindfulness and Meditation Practices:

Mindfulness and meditation are powerful tools for managing stress and improving mental clarity. Incorporating these practices into your daily routine can help you stay grounded and focused.

### 1-1 Mindfulness Techniques:

**Mindful Breathing:** Practice deep, mindful breathing to help center your thoughts and reduce anxiety. Focus on the sensation of your breath entering and leaving your body.

**Body Scan Meditation:** Perform a body scan meditation to become aware of physical sensations and release tension. This practice involves mentally scanning each part of your body, from head to toe, and noticing any sensations without judgment.

**Mindful Observation:** Take a few minutes each day to observe your surroundings mindfully. Focus on the sights, sounds, and smells around you, and practice being present in the moment.

## 1-2 Meditation Practices:

**Guided Meditation:** Use guided meditation apps like Headspace or Calm to help you get started with meditation. These apps offer various sessions tailored to different needs, such as stress reduction or improved focus.

**Silent Meditation:** Set aside time for silent meditation. Find a quiet space, sit comfortably, and focus on your breath or a mantra to help clear your mind.

**Loving-Kindness Meditation:** Practice loving-kindness meditation to cultivate compassion and empathy. This involves silently repeating phrases of goodwill towards yourself and others.

## 2-Physical Exercise for Stress Reduction:

Regular physical exercise is essential for maintaining mental health. Exercise releases endorphins, which help reduce stress and improve mood.

## 2-1 Incorporating Exercise into Your Routine:

**Daily Workouts:** Aim to include at least 30 minutes of moderate exercise in your daily routine. This could be a morning jog, a midday yoga session, or an evening workout.

**Short Break Exercises:** Use breaks throughout your day to perform short exercises. This can include stretching, a quick walk, or desk exercises to keep your body active.

**Online Fitness Classes:** Participate in online fitness classes to stay motivated and accountable. Many platforms offer a wide range of classes, from high-intensity interval training (HIIT) to Pilates and dance workouts.

## 2-2 Types of Exercise:

**Aerobic Exercise:** Engage in aerobic activities like running, cycling, or swimming to boost cardiovascular health and reduce anxiety.

**Strength Training:** Incorporate strength training exercises, such as weight lifting or bodyweight exercises, to build muscle and improve overall fitness.

**Flexibility and Balance:** Practice activities that enhance flexibility and balance, such as yoga or tai chi. These exercises can help reduce physical tension and improve mental focus.

## 3-Healthy Eating and Sleep Hygiene:

Nutrition and sleep play crucial roles in mental health and well-being. Maintaining a balanced diet and good sleep hygiene can significantly impact your mood and energy levels.

## 3-1 Healthy Eating Habits:

**Balanced Diet:** Consume a balanced diet rich in fruits, vegetables, whole grains, lean proteins, and healthy fats. Proper nutrition supports brain function and energy levels.

**Hydration:** Stay hydrated by drinking plenty of water throughout the day. Dehydration can lead to fatigue and decreased concentration.
**Mindful Eating:** Practice mindful eating by paying attention to the taste, texture, and aroma of your food. Avoid eating in front of screens to fully engage with your meals.

## 3-2 Sleep Hygiene Practices:
**Consistent Sleep Schedule:** Maintain a regular sleep schedule by going to bed and waking up at the same time each day, even on weekends.
**Sleep Environment:** Create a sleep-friendly environment by keeping your bedroom cool, dark, and quiet. Use comfortable bedding and limit exposure to screens before bedtime.
**Relaxation Techniques:** Incorporate relaxation techniques into your bedtime routine, such as reading, listening to calming music, or practicing gentle stretches.

## 4-Building and Maintaining Social Connections:

Social connections are vital for mental health. Staying connected with friends, family, and colleagues can provide emotional support and reduce feelings of isolation.

## 4-1 Staying Connected Virtually:
**Regular Check-Ins:** Schedule regular check-ins with friends and family through video calls, phone calls, or messaging apps. These interactions can provide a sense of normalcy and support.

**Virtual Social Events:** Participate in virtual social events, such as online game nights, book clubs, or virtual coffee breaks with colleagues. These activities can help maintain social bonds and provide enjoyment.

## 4-2 Creating Support Networks:
**Professional Networks:** Engage with professional networks and online communities related to your field. This can provide opportunities for networking, learning, and support.

**Mental Health Support Groups:** Join mental health support groups, either online or in-person, to connect with others who may be experiencing similar challenges. These groups can offer valuable insights and encouragement.

## 5-Practicing Gratitude and Positive Thinking:

Cultivating gratitude and maintaining a positive mindset can significantly enhance your mental health. These practices help shift focus away from negative thoughts and foster a sense of contentment.

## 5-1 Gratitude Practices:
**Daily Gratitude Journal:** Keep a daily gratitude journal where you write down things you are thankful for each day. Reflecting on positive aspects of your life can boost your mood and outlook.

**Expressing Gratitude:** Take time to express gratitude to others. This could be through a thank-you note, a kind message, or verbally acknowledging someone's support.

## 5-2 Positive Thinking Techniques:

**Positive Affirmations:** Use positive affirmations to reinforce self-belief and confidence. Repeat affirmations daily to build a positive self-image.

**Reframing Negative Thoughts:** Practice reframing negative thoughts by focusing on positive outcomes or lessons learned. This helps shift your perspective and reduces stress.

Enhancing mental health and well-being is essential for thriving in a remote work environment. By incorporating mindfulness and meditation practices, regular physical exercise, healthy eating and sleep hygiene, and maintaining social connections, you can significantly improve your mental health. Additionally, cultivating gratitude and positive thinking can further support your emotional well-being. In the next chapter, we will explore strategies for staying connected and engaged with your team and colleagues, ensuring effective communication and collaboration in a remote work setting.

# CHAPTER 9: STAYING CONNECTED AND ENGAGED

Maintaining strong connections and staying engaged with your team is crucial for the success of remote work. Without the physical presence of colleagues, remote workers can often feel isolated, which can impact morale and productivity. This chapter will provide strategies for building and maintaining virtual relationships, utilizing effective communication tools, and engaging in virtual team-building activities to foster a cohesive and motivated remote team.

## 1-Building Virtual Relationships:
Creating and nurturing relationships in a remote work environment requires intentional effort. Strong relationships contribute to better teamwork, collaboration, and overall job satisfaction.

## 1-1 Regular Check-Ins:
**One-on-One Meetings:** Schedule regular one-on-one meetings with team members to discuss progress, provide feedback, and address any concerns. These meetings help build trust and rapport.
**Team Meetings:** Hold regular team meetings to keep everyone updated on project progress, share news, and encourage team collaboration. Use these meetings to reinforce team goals and values.

## 1-2 Personal Connections:
**Virtual Coffee Breaks:** Set up virtual coffee breaks where team members can chat informally. These casual interactions help replicate the spontaneous conversations that occur in an office setting.

**Social Channels:** Create dedicated social channels in your communication platform (e.g., Slack, Microsoft Teams) for non-work-related discussions. This can include topics like hobbies, pets, or weekend plans.

### 1-3 Empathy and Support:

**Active Listening:** Practice active listening during conversations. Show genuine interest in your colleagues' experiences and challenges.

**Offer Support:** Be supportive and understanding of your team members' needs. Offer assistance and flexibility when they face personal or professional challenges.

## 2-Effective Communication Tools:

Leveraging the right communication tools is essential for staying connected and ensuring smooth collaboration in a remote work environment.

### 2-1 Video Conferencing:

**Tools:** Use video conferencing tools like Zoom, Microsoft Teams, or Google Meet for meetings. Video calls help mimic face-to-face interactions and enhance communication.

**Etiquette:** Follow video call etiquette, such as muting your microphone when not speaking, being punctual, and maintaining eye contact to show engagement.

## 2-2 Instant Messaging:

**Tools:** Utilize instant messaging platforms like Slack, Microsoft Teams, or WhatsApp for quick, real-time communication. These tools facilitate instant updates and casual conversations.

**Channels:** Create specific channels or groups for different projects, departments, or topics to keep conversations organized and focused.

## 2-3 Collaborative Platforms:

**Document Sharing:** Use platforms like Google Workspace or Microsoft Office 365 for document sharing and real-time collaboration. These tools allow multiple users to work on the same document simultaneously.

**Project Management:** Implement project management tools like Trello, Asana, or Monday.com to track tasks, deadlines, and project progress. These platforms provide transparency and keep everyone on the same page.

## 3-Virtual Team-Building Activities:

Engaging in virtual team-building activities can strengthen team bonds, boost morale, and improve collaboration.

## 3-1 Icebreaker Activities:

**Fun Questions:** Start meetings with fun icebreaker questions to lighten the mood and encourage team members to share more about themselves.

**Two Truths and a Lie:** Play simple games like "Two Truths and a Lie" where team members share two true statements and one false statement about themselves, and others guess which is the lie.

## 3-2 Collaborative Games:

**Online Escape Rooms:** Participate in online escape rooms that require team members to work together to solve puzzles and complete challenges within a set time.

**Virtual Trivia:** Organize virtual trivia games covering a range of topics. This can be a fun way to encourage friendly competition and team interaction.

## 3-3 Wellness Activities:

**Virtual Workouts:** Host virtual workout sessions or yoga classes. These activities promote physical health and provide a break from work-related discussions.

**Mindfulness Sessions:** Conduct virtual mindfulness or meditation sessions to help team members relax and reduce stress.

## 4-Encouraging Engagement and Participation:

Fostering an environment where team members feel valued and encouraged to participate actively is crucial for maintaining engagement.

## 4-1 Inclusive Practices:

**Solicit Feedback:** Regularly ask for feedback and suggestions from team members on how to improve workflows and team dynamics. This shows that their opinions are valued.

**Rotate Meeting Roles:** Rotate roles during meetings, such as note-taker, timekeeper, or facilitator, to involve different team members and encourage participation.

## 4-2 Recognition and Rewards:

**Celebrate Achievements:** Recognize and celebrate individual and team achievements, whether through shout-outs in meetings, virtual award ceremonies, or written acknowledgments.

**Incentives:** Offer incentives for meeting goals or milestones, such as gift cards, extra time off, or small tokens of appreciation.

## 4-3 Continuous Learning and Development:

**Professional Development:** Provide opportunities for professional development through online courses, webinars, or workshops. Encourage team members to share what they've learned with the team.

**Mentorship Programs:** Implement mentorship programs where more experienced team members can guide and support newer or less experienced colleagues.

Staying connected and engaged in a remote work environment requires deliberate effort and the right strategies. By building strong virtual relationships, utilizing effective communication tools, and participating in team-building activities, remote teams can maintain cohesion and productivity. Encouraging engagement and participation further ensures that team members feel valued and motivated. In the next chapter, we will explore how to manage workload and expectations effectively, providing strategies to set realistic goals, learn to say no, and seek support when needed.

# CHAPTER 10: MANAGING WORKLOAD AND EXPECTATIONS

Balancing workload and expectations is crucial for long-term success and well-being in a remote work environment. This chapter offers practical strategies for setting realistic goals, managing tasks effectively, and knowing when to seek support. By mastering these skills, you can enhance your productivity, maintain a healthy work-life balance, and achieve your professional goals.

## 1-Setting Realistic Goals and Deadlines:

Setting clear and achievable goals is essential for managing your workload effectively. Realistic goals help you stay focused, motivated, and on track.

## 1-1 SMART Goals:

**Specific:** Clearly define what you want to achieve. For example, instead of saying "improve productivity," specify "complete project X by Friday."

**Measurable:** Ensure your goal can be tracked and measured. Use metrics like time spent, tasks completed, or quality of output.

**Achievable:** Set goals that are challenging yet attainable. Consider your current workload, resources, and time constraints.

**Relevant:** Align your goals with your broader objectives and career aspirations.

Time-Bound: Set deadlines to maintain focus and urgency. Break larger goals into smaller tasks with individual deadlines.

## 1-2 Break Down Large Projects:

**Milestones:** Divide larger projects into smaller, manageable tasks. This makes the project less overwhelming and allows for incremental progress.

**Prioritization:** Focus on high-priority tasks first to ensure that the most critical elements are completed on time.

## 2-Learning to Say No:

Learning to say no is a vital skill for managing your workload and maintaining your well-being. It ensures that you don't overcommit and can focus on your priorities.

## 2-1 Assess Commitments:

**Evaluate Requests:** Before agreeing to take on new tasks, consider if they align with your goals and current workload.

**Set Boundaries:** Politely decline tasks that overextend your capacity. Respect your limits to prevent burnout.

## 2-2 Communicate Effectively:

**Be Honest:** Clearly explain why you cannot take on additional work. Honesty fosters understanding and respect.

**Offer Alternatives:** Suggest other resources or timelines when declining requests. This shows willingness to help while maintaining your boundaries.

## 3-Building a Support Network:

A strong support network is vital for remote work success. Both professional and personal support systems can provide valuable assistance and encouragement.

### 2-1 Professional Support:
**Mentorship:** Seek advice from mentors or colleagues. They can offer valuable insights, guidance, and feedback based on their experiences.
**Peer Networks:** Join professional groups and networks to connect with peers who share similar challenges and can offer support and advice.

### 2-2 Personal Support:
**Friends and Family:** Lean on friends and family for emotional support. Sharing your challenges and successes can help alleviate stress and boost morale.
**Community Groups:** Engage with community groups or online forums related to your field to share experiences and gain new perspectives.

## 3-Effective Delegation and Outsourcing:

Knowing when and how to delegate tasks can help you manage your workload more effectively and focus on high-priority activities.

### 3-1 Delegation Strategies:
**Team Collaboration:** Delegate tasks to team members who have the capacity and skills to handle them. This allows you to focus on higher-priority tasks and leverage your team's strengths.

**Clear Instructions:** Provide clear instructions and expectations when delegating tasks to ensure that they are completed correctly and efficiently.

## 3-2 Outsourcing:

**Freelancers and Vendors:** Consider outsourcing tasks that can be handled by freelancers or external vendors. This can be particularly useful for specialized tasks that require specific expertise.

**Cost-Benefit Analysis:** Evaluate the cost and benefits of outsourcing to ensure that it provides value and helps you manage your workload effectively.

As we wrap up this guide, remember that managing workload and expectations is an ongoing process that requires constant attention and adjustment. Embrace flexibility, seek support when needed, and celebrate your successes along the way. With the strategies and insights provided in this book, you are well-equipped to navigate the challenges of remote work and achieve a fulfilling, balanced, and productive work life. Stay committed to your growth and continue to adapt and thrive in your remote work journey.

# CONCLUSION

As you have journeyed through this book, you've likely noticed certain pieces of advice appearing more than once, such as the importance of good sleep, maintaining a healthy diet, and regular exercise. These recurring themes highlight the foundational elements of a successful remote work lifestyle. They are the pillars that support your overall well-being and productivity.

However, this repetition doesn't mean that the topics mentioned only once are any less important. Each chapter offers unique insights and strategies that contribute to a holistic approach to managing remote work. Every aspect, from setting realistic goals to building a support network, plays a crucial role in creating a balanced and fulfilling remote work experience.

By integrating these diverse strategies, you can tailor your remote work routine to fit your personal needs and professional goals. Continuous improvement and adaptability are key to thriving in this dynamic environment.

For further reading and to expand your knowledge on achieving a balanced and aesthetic lifestyle, I highly recommend exploring my series on holistic wellness. Specifically, check out "Sleep Smarter: Natural Strategies for Better Rest and Well-Being" for an in-depth guide on optimizing your sleep, and "Wake Up Winning: Master Your Morning, Transform Your Life" for strategies to kickstart your day with energy and focus. These books provide detailed insights into creating effective routines that enhance both your personal and professional life.

Thank you for dedicating your time to this book. I hope the strategies and insights shared here empower you to master remote work and achieve a fulfilling, productive, and balanced life. Stay committed to your growth, embrace flexibility, and continue to thrive on your remote work journey.

Remember, the journey towards mastering remote work is ongoing, and with the right approach, you can achieve lasting success and well-being.

May you find peace in every morning coffee, control in every problem, and in the end, may you find aesthetic.

# BIBLIOGRAPHY

**1-**"Remote: Office Not Required" by Jason Fried and David Heinemeier Hansson
**Publisher:** Crown Business, 2013

**2-**"The Year Without Pants: WordPress.com and the Future of Work" by Scott Berkun
**Publisher:** Jossey-Bass, 2013

**3-**"Deep Work: Rules for Focused Success in a Distracted World" by Cal Newport
**Publisher:** Grand Central Publishing, 2016

**4-**"Atomic Habits: An Easy & Proven Way to Build Good Habits & Break Bad Ones" by James Clear
**Publisher:** Avery, 2018

**5-**"The 4-Hour Workweek: Escape 9-5, Live Anywhere, and Join the New Rich" by Timothy Ferriss
**Publisher:** Crown Archetype, 2007

**6-**"Essentialism: The Disciplined Pursuit of Less" by Greg McKeown
**Publisher:** Crown Business, 2014

www.ingramcontent.com/pod-product-compliance
Lightning Source LLC
Chambersburg PA
CBHW050234230526
45470CB00005B/1940